Projects for the Mini Lathe

Dick Sing

Text written with and
photography by Donna S. Baker

Schiffer Publishing Ltd®
880 Lower Valley Road, Atglen, PA 19310 USA

M000276935

Dedication

To Eileen Young
my favorite mother-in-law
The lady who is the brunt of my joking during
demonstrations
such as to the man in front of the lathe,
"you are sitting in my mother-in-law's seat,"
or "I respect my mother-in-law,
how many women do you know who, at age 65,
go out and learn how to fly a broom?"
Thank you for being you.
Thank you for your daughter.

Copyright © 2002 by Dick Sing
Library of Congress Control Number: 2001094544

Designed by John P. Cheek
Cover design by Bruce M. Waters
Gallery set-up by Cindy Sing

Type set in ZapfHumanist Dm BT/ZapfHumanist BT

ISBN: 0-7643-1462-9
Printed in China

Published by Schiffer Publishing Ltd.
4880 Lower Valley Road
Atglen, PA 19310
Phone: (610) 593-1777; Fax: (610) 593-2002
E-mail: Schifferbk@aol.com
Please visit our web site catalog at **www.schifferbooks.com**
We are always looking for people to write books on new and related subjects. If you have an idea for a book, please contact us at the above address.

This book may be purchased from the publisher.
Include $3.95 for shipping.
Please try your bookstore first.
You may write for a free catalog.

In Europe, Schiffer books are distributed by
Bushwood Books
6 Marksbury Avenue
Kew Gardens
Surrey TW9 4JF England
Phone: 44 (0) 20 8392 8585
Fax: 44 (0) 20 8392 9876
E-mail: Bushwd@aol.com
Free postage in the UK. Europe: air mail at cost.

Contents

Introduction

A question I am frequently asked is: "What next after pens? Now that I have a mini lathe that I purchased for turning pens, I need another challenge. Pens were fun, but all of my friends and family now have them. Now what do I do?"

In response to this request, I have tried to put together a few projects that will increase your abilities and help make you a better turner. These are simple yet not so simple projects. They are meant to take you from basic small projects that let you expand your abilities to projects that help you overcome the challenge of holding the work piece by various methods.

When I am demonstrating, one of the things that intrigues people is how I hold things with what they consider to be unfamiliar and difficult to implement methods. Throughout these pages, I will endeavor to make this as painless as possible. Believe it or not, this can become fun and addictive. It can be very satisfying to reverse the piece, conquer difficult holding situations, add embellishment, combinations of materials, or multiple axis turnings. All of the situations that we will encounter can be applied to all aspects of turning, whether large or small.

Small projects demand a light touch and sharp tools, as well as good eye and hand coordination. Because of the small amount of material used, it is easier to go wrong for lack of surface area to work with. One small slip could totally destroy a bead. You need to take care and pride in the design, tooling, and finishing of your project.

I am sure a lot of turners will turn their nose up at the idea of toys, gadgets, or whatever derogatory name they can find to use for small projects. They want to do the big stuff, but what if you do not have a big lathe and all of the bells and whistles? You may have a summer home or travel trailer and it is easier to take along a smaller lathe as you can't leave your baby behind. What else would you do with all of that extra time but have fun and turn?

By doing the smaller things first you have little investment and will also develop a more refined skill to do large and more intricate projects. It is all proportional. Clean cutting on a small object demands dexterity and an understanding of how the tools work. When practicing on small projects, you have a smaller surface and smaller cuts that demand a light touch with sharp tools.

Another plus to using the mini lathe and smaller pieces of wood is that if a mistake is made it is not as costly. With mistakes on the mini lathe, the smaller work piece typically just falls to the floor. In contrast, a larger twenty pound work piece normally becomes a spinning missile which can cause major damage to yourself, others around you, or heaven forbid any of the tools in your shop.

With the small projects, you have to pay more attention to the details, as haphazard cutting can tear the surface beyond repair and easily dislodge the work piece. Just because the work piece is smaller does not justify any less effort to make it into a valued piece. I've included in this book a variety of tips and methods for taking what is at hand to develop your skills further. I make use of scrap blocks, double-face tape, jam chucks, drill chucks, and four jaw chucks to show how to mount, remount, reverse, or whatever it takes to accomplish your finished project. The mounting and remounting always seems to be a problem for people.

Double-face tape as a holding medium scares a lot of people, although it is one way to hold a work piece without marring the surface. With a little confidence, this can become one of your major problem solvers when it comes to securing difficult to hold pieces. Again, as with the small projects, it is an asset, because if it does separate no harm is done. If a piece is ruined the investment is minor. It's not rocket science. I will walk you through the process — all it takes is common sense and the spirit of adventure.

I personally enjoy small projects even though I do large bowls and platters. Everything you learn can definitely be applied to anything larger. Being large myself, I still enjoy the small things — my wife Cindy is only 5'2".

I will show you how the projects are designed to stir your imagination along with increasing your skills. I will also show you how a simple project can be expanded into multiple and complex designs. Follow my lead then go on from there.

One thing that I ask is please read the book. The pictures are nice and hopefully do tell a story, but there are a thousand words between them that create the whole picture.

Clip Magnets

If you are like me, you hate to throw away those scrap cutoffs or irregular pieces of really good wood. Some of it is just too pretty to be scrap. *Voila* — there is a use for those odds and ends of scrap material!

Magnetic memo clips are readily available with a colored plastic disk in the center that can be removed and replaced with a decorative piece of wood. You can now take a sterile looking clip and make it into a mini work of art.

Let's start by using one of those salvaged pieces to make a simple medallion that will be attached to the clip. Once we have achieved the basics, we can start to experiment and implement new designs and surface treatments. I will be adding beads, contours, and chatterwork along with combinations of materials for inlays. Hopefully as you move along, your own imagination will be stirred as was mine.

I am using a four jaw chuck with a scrap block. If you do not have a four jaw chuck, use a faceplate with a scrap block screwed to it. This is still versatile but not as fast to use. A scrap block is waste wood, or scrap that will be used to hold the work piece and can also be cut away to provide access to the piece you are working on after the bulk of the material is removed. One of the things I always do is mark the position of any scrap blocks or jigs that I make, including screw holes on faceplates. This helps to relocate them in the jaws so they are as concentric as possible if reused.

To start, we are going to make a simple medallion or wooden disk to fill the recess where the plastic disk was removed. The wood that we are using is a piece of desert ironwood with a combination of heartwood and sapwood. It has enough extra wood to ensure the proper diameter and thickness after being cleaned up. Of course, this should hold true in all turnings.

Our first step is to clean up the face of the scrap block so it is flat, as it will be used to hold double-face tape.

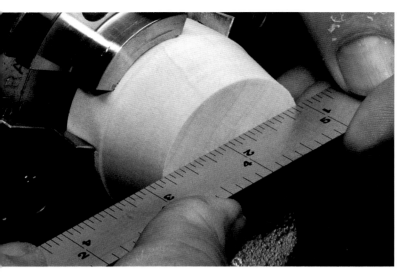

Make sure the surface is flat.

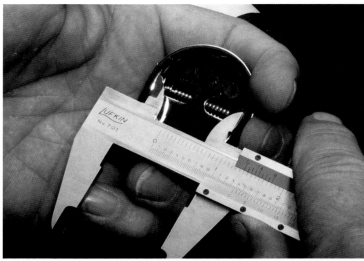

Using a vernier caliper or ruler, measure the recess in the clip.

In preparation, I had cleaned up the back of our wooden disk on a disk sander. This will give good adhesion to the tape. I have also applied a piece of double-face tape to the scrap block. Use a good quality tape as all double-face tapes are not created equal.

Clean up the surface and put on a rough line with a pencil for the diameter that we need.

I have applied our disk to the piece. Press securely and hold for a minute. This will help guarantee a better grip.

Reduce the excess waste towards the desired diameter. The tool that I am using is a 1/4" spindle gouge. A 3/8" spindle gouge would also work fine.

Cutting away the scrap block to give better accessibility to our work piece — this is what the scrap block is intended for.

I have reduced the thickness to what looks pleasing to the eye. When cutting this surface I normally use a shear cut so the pressure is going towards the headstock. A normal cut (large diameter to small diameter) can be used, but a light cut is a necessity. This helps to prevent dislodging the work piece from the tape.

I have also turned the disk to our desired diameter using a normal cut, again towards the headstock.

At the bottom of the clip's recess, the outside diameter has a radius. In order for the disk to set flat on the bottom of the clip, we need to cut a matching or larger radius on the mating surface. Again, the scrap block can be cut away to allow us to cut that radius.

Now that we have our piece basically turned, it's time to finish. Start sanding with the coarsest grit necessary to remove imperfections. Remove all defects before going on to the next grit. If you believe the next grit will eliminate imperfections left by the previous grit, you are wrong: the finer grit will only enhance the mistakes left by the previous grit. At times it is best to back up and remove those imperfections with the proper grit. If you find it necessary to use something in the neighborhood of 36 grit, my suggestion is to practice your cutting skills. The surface of my piece was good enough that I only needed to start with 240 grit sandpaper and end with 400. When you are satisfied with the sanding, stop the lathe and lightly sand with the grain to remove any concentric sanding marks.

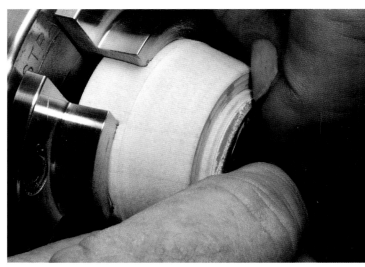

When removing your work piece from the scrap block, the secret is to apply pressure and hold it. This allows the tape to relax slowly so you can separate the work piece from the scrap block without damaging the work piece (such as cracking the thin disk).

Before gluing the disk into the magnet I like to take a soft wheel on a buffer with wax and give it a light buffing. To glue it in, I normally use silicone adhesive. You could also use the new flexible cyanoacrylate glue, although I would still prefer the silicone adhesive.

Next apply the finish of your choice. I am using Deft™ satin finish. Apply one coat and let set for a minute before wiping off the excess. Turn the lathe on (covering the work piece with a quality paper towel to keep your glasses clean!) and lightly buff. If you feel it necessary, you can apply additional coats following the same procedures. You can use any finish of your choice, such as friction polishes, oils, or even wax. I prefer the Deft as it does not give me a glossy finish and I prefer a softer, matte finish. The choice is yours.

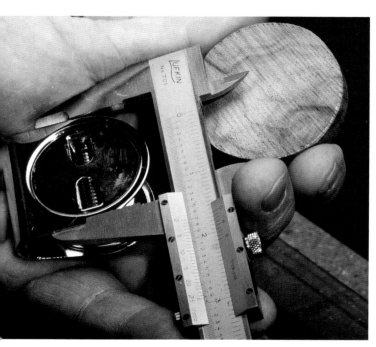

I have faced off the surface of the piece and marked the diameter of the recess.

The disk we just completed was simply located inside the recessed part of the clip. Next we will make a disk that is a little more challenging, as it will cover the entire circular part of the clip face. We will use a piece of figured walnut and I have cut it larger than the widest part of our clip. Our scrap block should still be OK as we did not harm the surface where the tape was attached. Apply the disk to the scrap block with the tape, just as we did for the first piece. I am still using my original tape—if you have had a problem or have gotten it dirty, just put on a new piece.

I am cutting a short tenon or offset that will match the recess of the clip.

I am trueing up the outside diameter to make sure we have enough stock, but do not take it to size.

Occasionally, place the clip on the disk and check for fit. This will insure a nice match of the wood to the metal and a good gluing surface. Once you have achieved this you can remove the disk from the scrap block. I do not bother to sand the surface as being slightly rough it gives a better adhesion for the glue. In all reality, this surface should probably be finished to help prevent it from warping, but I use dry wood and that has not become a problem.

Remove the tape and resurface the scrap block.

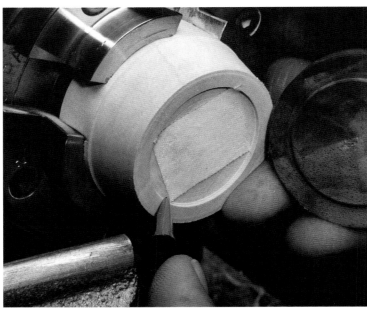

I have applied a piece of double-face tape to the bottom of the recess on the scrap block. We will then apply the disk to the tape, using the recess to center it. If you've cut the recess too large and have a lot of play or extra clearance, use a larger piece of tape that will extend up the walls. This will help to fill the gap and keep the disk more centered.

Mark out the determined diameter of the tenon. We are going to use the tenon to locate the disk to the scrap block so it will be concentric when we work on the opposite side, which will become the face.

Cut a recess into the scrap block that will match the tenon—depth and diameter wise. I am using a parting tool, but a square end flat scraper could be used as well. Continue until your match has been completed.

Apply the disk to the tape. The mounting is completed and we are now ready to turn the face. I am starting to work the face of our disk.

Reduce the diameter to the predetermined measurement of the width of the clip. We are now ready to embellish the face.

I am roughing in the face by adding a couple of beads.

Using the tip of the gouge, carefully roll the bead. Remember this is a delicate cut and it does not take a lot of error to ruin the surface. Strive to make clean cuts, rather than scraping.

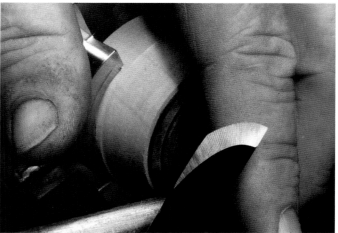

This tool may look like a skew, but the angle is approximately 65° included. I use this in a shear scraping mode although at times it's a blatant scrape, as I cannot get into a shear scraping position due to lack of working room. Most of the time, however, the tool is in a shearing mode. The French curve type shape gives me a multitude of surfaces to work with for various contours.

I am using the shear scraper type tool to clean up the surface between the beads. Be careful not to destroy any of your hard work on the beads.

11

This disk now matches the outside diameter of the clip and makes a larger and more decorative surface. I personally like the larger disk, even though it takes a bit more work to accomplish. Gluing the disk to the metal clip is done the same as previously.

This edge I want to keep sharp as it is going to match the metal surface of the clip. I also feel it will be more eye pleasing.

When sanding against beads, I like to use the edge of the sandpaper. This allows me to sand to the bead, rather than over it, which would destroy all the detail I have strived to put into it.

Seeing how we are going to make more disks, remove the scrap block from the chuck as we will use it again. Once you have a decent fit, there is no need to refit for each additional disk, as long as the dimensions are the same.

Our next disk is going to incorporate another element of surface decoration—chatterwork. In choosing the wood, we must have a hard, close grained species. Chatterwork is accomplished best on end grain, but on a piece this thin end grain would not be very strong so we have to use face grain. The wood I am using is desert ironwood because it has the characteristics needed. If we used a species such as pine, which is soft, it would tear the grain rather than cut it, making a total chaos of the surface. As long as we're experimenting, let's try another exercise in holding: we will use just the four jaw chuck. Normally the jaws are much deeper than our thin disk. To locate the disk on the face edges of the jaws so you can work on it, make a small spacer with the thickness depending on the jaw depth of your chuck. This will help position the disk parallel to the jaws and in its proper depth. I use just a small piece of double-face tape to keep the spacer centered to the work piece for convenience. This spacer can be eliminated by grabbing the disk with the edges of the jaws and careful positioning. I will be not using the spacer here but I do recommend its use if you have a problem setting up your work piece.

After sanding, I am finishing the disk, following the same procedure as before (or the one of your choice).

Once you have made a tenon to match the recess on the clip as we did previously, you can remove the disk from the chuck.

One of the challenges of using desert ironwood is its ability to have cracks where they were not visible prior to your first cut. This piece had such a crack that was not apparent earlier. Rather than discarding it, let's go through the process of fixing it.

Put the scrap block back in, remembering your jaw location marks. If you need to, replace the tape, then affix the disk to it as done previously.

Using water thin cyanoacrylate, flood the crack and apply accelerator.

Since we are using the same scrap block from our previous disk, the diameter has already been established on the scrap block. Face off your work piece.

Face off the glued surface and reassess the crack. This one is still slightly visible but given the nature of the beast the next piece of ironwood might be the same. Since we are going to put chatterwork on it—which will help camouflage the crack—let's give it a go. The worst scenario would be having to discard it after all, but going through the process provides valuable practice (which we could all probably use).

Start embellishing the face, adding a bead or whatever you like. Remember not to get too flowery so your embellishment doesn't overpower the chatterwork that is planned.

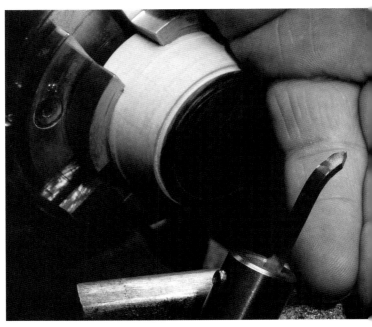

The chatter tool is basically composed of a heavy steel shaft with a piece of spring steel affixed in the end, which sets up harmonic vibrations when applied to the work. The only thing guaranteed in chatterwork is that you can get any pattern only once. You can achieve similar patterns but there are no guarantees. The speed of the lathe, the composition of the wood, the height of the tool rest, the pressure you apply on the tool, the angle of the tool to the wood, the direction of travel, and your mother's hat size all have a bearing on how the pattern will evolve. The best way to understand the chatter tool is through practice. Put a length of wood in the chuck with end grain showing for the face—use hard maple or some other close grained hardwood. This will give you your best patterns so you can see and understand what happens. Vary the lathe speed, tool rest height, pressure applied to the work piece, directional changes, or anything else you can think of that may give you a different pattern. Stop the lathe, study your results and remember how you achieved them, then take a tool, erase the pattern, and do it again. It won't take long for you to get the drift of how it works. How well you retain this in the real world, depends on you. Don't be discouraged if your first results aren't up to your expectations— consider it a challenge to improve. It can become fun!

Sand your disk. Before any chatterwork is done, the surface must be sanded to finished quality, as chatterwork will not hide sanding scratches or imperfections in the surface. Proper preparation of the surface will give you the best chatterwork results.

With the chatter tool positioned on the tool rest, the spring steel tool end must be unsupported. This is where all the vibration comes from. If you put the spring end on the tool rest, it stops all the vibration and basically becomes a dead issue.

Apply the chatter tool to the surface with a smooth, uniform movement.

Now lightly burnish the surface with 400 grit sandpaper. This will enhance the surface and show you your pattern. If you are content with the pattern you have achieved, go on to the next step. If not, erase it and try again. And if needed, keep trying—until you run out of wood!

Using a small V-point scraper, I like to go in next and detail the edges. This just makes a nice, clean, crisp surface around the edges of the chatterwork. Do this carefully, as you do not want to continue the chatterwork across the remainder of the piece in the form of a spiral or catch.

The finished chatterwork magnet. Notice that between the glue repair and the chatterwork that was applied, the crack we found earlier is no longer discernible.

Next we will make a medallion with inlays. The woods I am going to use will be koa, for the outer ring; maple, for the accent ring; and manzanita root, for the center. You can distinguish the three woods by their sizes in the picture. I chose these woods because I thought their colorations and contrast complemented each other well. Normally, you would not want all dark woods or all light woods, which would not show the contrast. My diameter for the outer ring will be 1-3/4", which is the large diameter of the magnet clip. The accent ring will be 1-1/4" diameter, with the center ring 1-1/8" diameter. By looking at these diameters, you can see that the accent ring will end up 1/16" wide. I chose these dimensions because the outer ring diameter was set by the clip. The accent ring was chosen strictly by my eye for proportion. The inner inlay was then dimensioned to give me a 1/16" accent ring. The thickness of each piece individually is approximately 5/16". This can vary as your scrap pieces, or whatever you use, will dictate. They will end up approximately 1/8" thick, which will be in proportion to the clip. If all this is confusing, follow along and I'll explain as we go.

In preparation, put a scrap block in the chuck and face off the front surface. Now cut out your inner disk (using a band saw or whatever you choose), disk sand the back surface, and attach to the scrap block with double-face tape. Start reducing the diameter down to the 1-1/8" dimension.

When you have attained the 1-1/4" diameter, you are ready to start making the inlaid medallion.

Work your diameter down to the 1-1/8" dimension, taking care to keep it parallel. The closer we make it, the more precise the fit between the inlays will be, by minimizing any possible gap. Once you have completed this, remove the piece and set aside.

Take the scrap block out, then take the remaining piece and center it in the jaws. Allow enough material to protrude to make a tenon that matches the clip, as in the previous projects. I am holding this in the chuck by its circumference, as we will be drilling a hole through its entirety. It could also be glued onto a scrap block, making sure that the outer diameter was glued securely.

Affix the accent piece to the same scrap block and start reducing it to the 1-1/4" diameter. Remember to always cut towards the headstock if possible. I've mentioned this before, but it's an important point to remember.

I will be using a 1-1/4" Fostner drill bit to cut the diameter for the accent inlay. Do not forget to slow down your lathe, as Fostner bits will burn if run at too high an rpm. Also remember we are using hardwoods, which will burn even easier.

Remove the chuck from the spindle and stand it upright. Insert the accent ring, taking care not to disturb the position of the outside ring in the chuck.

Drill through the piece, taking care as you penetrate the back side. This will help prevent tear out on the back side (which will become the face side on our completed inlay).

Flood the joint line with the water thin cyanoacrylate and apply accelerator. The main reason I remove the chuck from the lathe is to place the inlays in a horizontal position. This allows me to flood the joint line and have it penetrate down through the entire joint.

The drilling is completed.

After the glue has cured, drill through the accent inlay.

Again remove the chuck from the lathe, stand upright, and insert the remaining inner inlay. Glue using the same process as before.

I have completed drilling through the accent inlay. The reason we are taking the steps in this sequence is that we now have a uniform 1/16" accent around our last hole. By not removing anything from the jaws of the chuck during this process, all of our inlays will remain concentric to each other. If you had tried to do this on a drill press without some kind of elaborate setup, chances are the drill bit would walk off in the direction of least resistance and create an uneven accent ring.

Face off the piece.

Cutting the tenon for the clip depression.

Clean up the face so we can see what we really have and bring our diameter close to the finished dimension.

We've fit the tenon to the clip.

Start to embellish the surface. I am going to form a bead on the outer diameter.

Remove the insert from the chuck and reinstall your scrap block with the matching recess. Use a piece of double-face tape to attach the insert to the scrap block.

Using the shear tool or a shear cut with the gouge, make a pleasant contour on the face.

Using the tip of a small spindle gouge, roll and detail a bead on the outer diameter.

Sand as normal, then check with the mirror and make adjustments as necessary.

Again using your favorite finish, finish to your satisfaction. One thing to remember – we're now making miniature works of art. Finish and detailing should reflect that. We are gaining experience and trying to improve constantly.

The finished inlay magnet.

Bolos

Some of your previous medallions have now reached the status of being too worthy to hang on a refrigerator. Next, the knowledge and skill you have acquired in turning the medallions can be applied to a similar project. After seeing your latest masterpieces, surely your mate, a family member, or a friend will voice the desire for a bolo. The difference between these and the magnets will be the addition of a recess on the back that will hold the cord clip and maybe a difference in size. With this project, colors and textures of wood are looked at for their ability to accessorize an outfit versus being seen as a clip that adorns a refrigerator door. Let's do it, and take on this new challenge.

The woods I am using will be Brazilian rosewood (which I have had for thirty years) as the outer ring, maple as the accent, and Chechen burl as the center. These woods were chosen from earth tones with color coordination to apparel in mind. When choosing yours, I'm sure the person you're intending the bolo for (which could be a man or woman since bolos are unisex) has certain favorite colors. Choose your woods accordingly. Also the textures of the woods, the chatoyancy (reflection of light like a cat's eye), plus the wood grain all contribute to the final product. In preparation, I have turned the accent inlay to a diameter of 1-5/8" and the center inlay to a diameter of 1-1/2"; the outer ring has not yet been turned. The diameters were turned on a scrap block with double-face tape as we did in the previous project. The difference between this project and the previous one will be that we need to finish both sides and have a recess on the back side for a cord clip. Also, on the previous project our inlays went completely through each other. On this one, however, we are going to have the back and side of the large diameter unbroken. Let's also try a different approach in chucking, since one of the principles of this book is learning how to handle different chucking situations.

Put a scrap block in the chuck large enough to accommodate the outer ring and face off the surface. Apply some medium density cyanoacrylate to the scrap block, put a little accelerator on the outer ring and immediately center it on the scrap block, rotating slightly to spread the glue. Then apply pressure. If you have waited too long, you can see that this instruction is unnecessary. One of the reasons I am gluing the piece to the scrap block is that it will provide strength to the back of the work piece while boring the holes. For some turners, it will also provide some extra holding security along with helping to learn a new chucking technique.

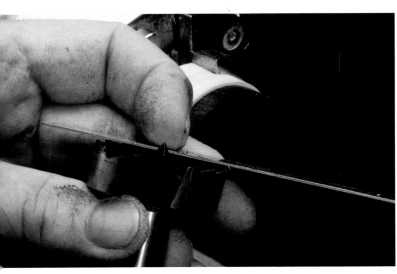

One of the problems with Fostner type bits and the project we are doing is that the center point of the bit would protrude through the back of the bolo if we drilled to the depth we wanted. We will only drill a short distance in to establish our desired diameter. Or you can measure and bore with the scraper, which I normally do.

As you can see, the bottom of the scraper has been relieved, to provide clearance. If it is not relieved, the bottom of the tool would possibly hit before the cutting edge. We still may have to use this tool slightly above center line to make sure this doesn't happen, especially on smaller diameter holes. When using a scraper, proper presentation is normally at or slightly below center line.

I used the 1-5/8" drill to lightly spot my hole. This marks our diameter exactly.

Using the scraper, bore the hole parallel to the ways. To do this, sight down the length of your tool and make sure it's running parallel to the ways. Strive to keep the bottom flat. My work piece is 5/16" thick and I am boring 1/8" deep.

I am going to finish the depth of the hole with a square end scraper. A parting tool can also be used as long as the hole is large enough that the top and bottom edges of the tool do not foul out on the edges of the hole.

Using the accent ring, fit it or keep trying it until it nests snugly in the hole.

When the accent ring fits, remove the chuck and again stand on end so you can glue in the accent piece. The accent ring was also 5/16" thick. Being inlaid 1/8" allows me a way of holding and removing the accent ring in preparation for gluing. Using the medium density cyanoacrylate, make sure the walls are glued, rotating for even coverage. The very center does not need to be glued, as we will be boring this out.

Using a 1-1/2" Fostner bit, spot the hole for the center inlay.

Put the chuck back on the lathe and face off the accent ring.

Using the scraper, again bore the depression, the same as we did for the accent ring.

If you've done it right, you should have no gaps between the two pieces.

Remove the chuck and make sure of your fit between the accent ring and the center inlay.

23

Prior to gluing, pay attention to the way the grain patterns are laid. Sometimes opposing grains will stand out very contrastingly; occasionally they will blend together. Make a mental note of this. Now, using the medium density cyanoacrylate, make sure the wall—and this time the bottom—has glue, rotating the inlay to spread the glue. Position the direction of the inlay to the preference you noted before gluing. Before hitting with accelerator, run a thin bead of water thin glue around both joint lines (accent and center inlay). This will allow the thin glue to run down into any cracks or voids that we may missed with the heavier glue. Spray with accelerator.

Put the chuck on the lathe and start to clean up the face.

Remember that your inlays are only 1/8" deep so treat the surface accordingly and don't remove too much.

I am rolling a bead the width of the accent ring. By making the edges of the bead in the joint lines, this can be used as a camouflaging technique in case you do not have a good fit between the joints. This is not the reason that I am doing it, however—I simply think it looks neat.

The edges and the face are ready for sanding. I used the point of the gouge to make a sharp corner at the bottom of the bead, inside and outside, to make it look crisp.

I have now sanded the bolo and applied finish. Our next step will be to remove it from the waste block.

Facing off the scrap block in preparation for making a jam chuck that will hold our bolo so we can finish the back side.

Using a sharp parting tool, part off on the waste block. Again, this is what a waste block is meant for. We are not cutting away any material from the bolo.

I have marked out the diameter of the bolo and am starting to relieve the face for clearance of the bolo.

We have parted off the bolo from the waste block and now need to finish the back side.

Using a drill, or a 3/8" spindle gouge as I am using here, bore a hole through the scrap block. Any time you make a jam chuck you may end up having a problem dislodging or removing the work piece from the chuck. By putting a hole through it, we will be able to push the piece back out if necessary (I suggest using a pencil with an eraser tip on an item like this so as not to mar the surface). If this were not done and it was a very tight fit, chances are you would have to cut away the scrap block to remove the work piece. Get in the habit of doing this all the time as it can save you a lot of needless heartaches.

Start to make a recess for the outside diameter of the bolo.

Our accent bead protrudes above the stopping surface, or the outside diameter of the bolo. Make sure that you relieve the corresponding bead and inner inlay surface of the scrap block to provide clearance for the bolo. We only want to contact on the outside diameter and face of the rosewood ring.

I have relieved the center of the scrap block to provide clearance for the curved face of the bolo. The outside diameter will provide the holding of the work piece. The wall must be as parallel as possible—align your cutting tool parallel to the ways to help achieve this. This is strictly a trial and error fit. The recess does not need to be very deep. A jam chuck will hold a work piece by its largest diameter. The holding strength is the same whether the recess is 1/8" or 1" deep. If the outer diameter of the bolo is parallel and finished, as mine is, we only need to hold it by approximately half its thickness. This will allow us to work the back side and the very edge, if necessary.

Testing frequently, work until you obtain a friction fit. Just this friction fit will provide enough holding power to work the back side of the bolo. Occasionally, we may err and make the recess larger than the work piece. You have a couple of options if this happens. Cover the recess with a paper towel or a sheet of toilet paper, depending on the amount of undesired clearance. Then seat the piece for a snug fit. If you have gone so far that this won't work, I suggest you try a new scrap block or face off the block you are using (if there is enough material) and cut another recess.

The flat surface that I am pointing to is very important. It will be a stop that will keep the bolo parallel to the face of the chuck.

This is what the inside of the scrap block looks like when it is properly fitted and clearanced. Yours may vary according to your surface embellishment or whatever your shape dictates.

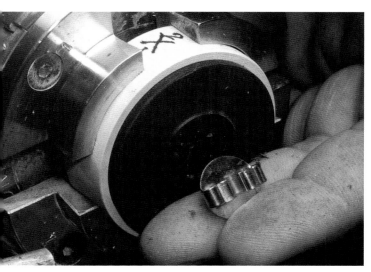

Press the bolo into the jam chuck, making sure the workpiece is held securely. We now need to cut a recess to accommodate the bolo cord clip.

We are finished with our recess and fitting of the clip. This serves a couple of purposes. It centers the clip to the bolo, covers the edge of the clip so glue is not exposed, and makes it look as though a little thought was put into the making of the bolo.

Using a parting tool or scraper, start to cut the recess for the clip, approximately the same thickness as the clip itself.

My piece has been sanded and finished, as we discussed on previous projects. The clip and bolo cord can be obtained from craft shops or places that carry jewelry findings. It should be glued in with silicone adhesive or flexible cyanoacrylate. Epoxy can be used but I feel it becomes brittle with time. Silicone adhesive or the flexible cyanoacrylate remain slightly pliable, which I feel gives a better shock resistant adhesion.

I am rolling a bead on the edge, strictly for aesthetics.

Here's the front of our completed bolo.

Offset Bolos

Now that we have mastered concentric inlays, let's advance our education and get into offset inlays. Using an offset or eccentric chuck can create patterns limited only by your imagination. About the time you think you have exhausted all the possibilities, you may come out of a sound sleep at 2:00 in the morning with yet another possibility in your mind.

People are often afraid of something they don't understand, but the only way to conquer this fear is to learn by doing. The first time I tried using offset turnings, not all was rosy. Being a bull headed individual, I have improved. There are still many aspects to be learned, however. I will endeavor to teach you a simple, basic technique for an offset bolo.

This chuck will be held by a four jaw chuck using the dovetailed recess. Any chuck with a dovetailed jaw capacity of 2-3/4" should hold it. There are three screws that hold on the scrap block. I am pointing to the concentric position. This is positioned with a screw. We have the option of going four holes to the left or four holes to the right. We also have the option of starting our initial turning at any of the holes and moving towards the remaining holes. Another option would be to rotate the scrap block at increments of 120° by removing the three screws holding the scrap block and repositioning the block to the existing screw holes. If you do this, prepare the scrap block with this in mind. Make sure it sets flat and the screw holes have been centered to the chuck and countersunk to the best of your ability. This will make all three holes as uniform as possible. Use caution and slow down the speed of your lathe. Being offset, the chuck is very out of balance and if run too fast could become a real problem. Safety first! If you are going to err, err on the slow side. Let's start—I will do my best to explain the functions as we go.

This offset chuck incorporates the use of a scrap block. In its present position, it is concentric.

We have mounted the offset chuck onto our four jaw chuck and faced off the scrap block.

Gluing the center inlay to the scrap block. I'm gluing the center rather than the outer ring to allow me design options. By doing this, I can do anything on the center ring, including a half circle inlay at the outer edge, trimming it back before banding it with a solid outer ring. We want to complete all of our inlays on the center piece because the center piece may change in diameter, have overlapping inlays, or something else – we don't know yet. The outer ring will have to be made to cover whatever design we have created on the center piece. I want the outer ring to be a solid band around the center piece. The woods I am using will be ebony, for both the outer ring and an accent ring; redheart, for the center; Bolivian rosewood for the largest inlay; and box elder burl for the smallest inlay.

> **TIP:** When laying out for inlay blanks, use a mechanical drawing circle template. This template has multiple size holes, which can be laid over figured wood so you can see exactly what your inlay will look like. This will help to use the figure of the wood to your best advantage.

Lightly face off the surface and roughly mark out the diameter you intend to use for the center piece. Mine happens to be 1-5/8". This is with the chuck in the concentric position.

I am in the process of laying out my piece for the inlays. My first inlay will be with the chuck moved one position clockwise and will be 1-1/4" in diameter.

I have moved the chuck to the second position clockwise and drawn in a 7/8" diameter inlay. Notice by my finger how the chuck is offset.

With the chuck returned to its first offset position, we will drill the hole for the largest inlay, which happens to be 1-1/4" in diameter. We will just spot the recess, being careful not to go through the back, as discussed with the previous bolo. The finished depth will be 1/8". Having determined all necessary diameters, I have precut my pieces on a scrap block with double-face tape, as previously discussed. Using a square edge scraper, finish the recess and glue in the ebony accent piece.

Next I am using a 1-1/8" Fostner bit to spot drill for the next inlay. Do not change the position of the chuck, as we want the accent ring to be concentric with this inlay. Cut to the depth of the accent ring.

After facing off my inlay, I am moving the eccentric chuck one more position, which will be two positions in the clockwise direction.

This picture shows how I want my grain alignment to be in order to best enhance the inlay. I have marked both pieces for reference. Glue in the inlay.

Now I have spotted and drilled a recess for the smallest inlay, again taking it down to 1/8" depth.

I've completed drilling for the last inlay. Glue it in, using the same process as before.

Return the eccentric chuck back to its original concentric position, which is two positions counterclockwise.

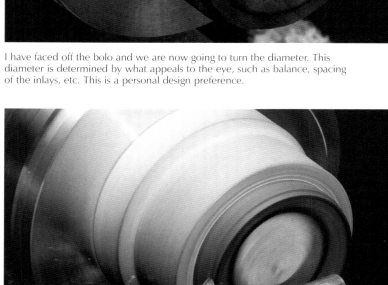

I have faced off the bolo and we are now going to turn the diameter. This diameter is determined by what appeals to the eye, such as balance, spacing of the inlays, etc. This is a personal design preference.

Reducing the diameter.

I've reduced the diameter down close to my needed dimension. I am going to leave it a little heavy in case the outer ring has an oversized hole. This will allow me a little latitude for adjustment.

Clean up the outer diameter and face off the inlays of the bolo.

I have taken the eccentric chuck off and set up the outer ring in the four jaw chuck. I'm drilling a 1-5/8" hole all the way through. This was determined by my finished, inlaid center pattern.

I am reducing the diameter of the outer ring to what looks best to me.

When this is completed, put the eccentric chuck back on and fit the outer ring over the inlays. If you take care, you should have a piece that fits tightly without gaps. Remove the chuck, stand on end, apply water thin glue around the joint, and allow to penetrate through the cracks.

After sanding my bolo, I am applying the finish.

Upon completing a project that used a scrap block, one of my habits is to always face it off in preparation for the next project.

Here's the finished bolo front before being removed from the scrap block.

Part off the bolo from the scrap block.

In preparation for the back side of the bolo, I have put the jam chuck block from the previous bolo back in the four jaw chuck. As Murphy's Law would have it, they never fit, so I am recutting it to fit the current bolo.

I have my piece in the jam chuck and am cleaning off the back side in preparation for the bolo clip.

On this bolo, I have just fitted the bolo clip in with no decoration around it. Sometimes simplicity works best.

TIP: Sometimes when applying cyanoacrylate, you want to control it, but given the nature of the beast it wants to run all over the place. I use a small piece of polyethylene packing material to spread the glue. The glue does not get on your fingers because it does not penetrate the material. If your polyethylene piece is too dirty, however, the contamination may set off the glue before you're ready. Another aspect of cyanoacrylate is that the tips of the bottle plug up very easily. This is normally caused by contamination when the tip contacts the work. The normal fix seems to be cutting back the tip, which leaves a larger hole. I have extra tips on hand, so when this happens, I remove the contaminated tip, put on a clean one, and throw the other tip into a small bottle of acetone. The acetone will dissolve the glue in time, leaving you a next-to-new tip. Extra tips are available. I have many tips from new bottles that I have never used as I continue to recycle the old ones. Another factor in contaminating the tips is putting the cap back on. Once I remove the cap, I leave it off unless I am transporting the bottle. If you buy your glue more than one bottle at a time, you can put an unopened bottle in the freezer to prolong its life. If you open it, do not go back to the freezer or you will contaminate it.

Here is the completed bolo. If things happen to you like they do to me, plain bolo cords are not satisfactory. To complete my bolo cords, I have made small wooden acorns or ornaments to put on the ends. I will have to admit this certainly is better than the metal aglet. All that is necessary would be to drill a hole for the cord in a blank and turn it on a dowel the same size as the hole. Several of these are shown in the gallery at the end of this book.

Earrings

And now, having created a monster, earrings need to be added to our bolo. After all, we aim to please: If momma's happy, you're happy. Let's try our skills at book-matching a pair of earrings.

Book matching is taking a piece of wood and splitting it through to the center, then separating it as if you were opening the pages of a book.

After opening, use the plastic circle template to lay out the blanks so the grain pattern is oriented in a mirror image. This will produce a matched pair. Using this method will show that thought went into the process, rather than relying on a random or haphazard layout.

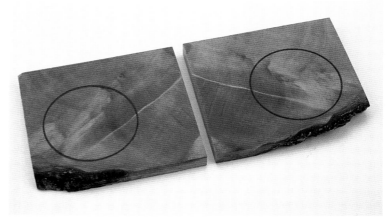

A set with a bolo and matched earrings. The same materials are used, the only difference is that the earrings are scaled down proportionally. One of the problems I was confronted with was the location of the post for the earring. Originally I had put them in the center, which was very simple. But they did not hang from my wife's ears the way she wanted. She wanted the post located closer to the rim.

To overcome spot drilling the back of a crowned earring, I had to make a jig. The jig consists of nothing more than a jam chuck with a flat bottom (against the chuck face), so it can stand on the drill press table.

The jig allows me to take the earring to the drill press and spot the location for the post. This spot allows the post to set flat to the surface and helps when gluing in.

The post in its position.

Rare-Earth Magnets

You have to use a rare-earth magnet to appreciate its strength. Because of their small size and powerful strength, they can be incorporated into small projects with a big hold. In this project, we will make decorative magnets to be used on any metal surface. Parents and grandparents are sure to enjoy these when their favorite little rugrat brings them a work of art to display. Being proud grandparents, my wife and I speak from experience — our refrigerator fell over on its side in the middle of the night due to all the artwork displayed on it by our grandsons, Collin and Jacob.

This different style of magnet can be fun and challenging as there are a multitude of ways to create and decorate them. I will share with you some of my ideas. We'll even show off a bit by adding a captive ring to wow your friends with. This is another skill for you to conquer and add to your repertoire.

I have mounted the piece of granadillo in the chuck and cleaned up the face.

Choosing the material. There are two ways to make these: using either face grain or end grain. The piece in the middle is end grain bocote. This type of wood looks very good showing end grain. If you are doing many of these, you could make a cylinder and cut them off in a series. The dark piece on the bottom is a piece of blistered figured granadillo and the light colored piece at the top is madrone. The two end pieces will probably make better face grain knobs as they will show off flash and figure. The diameters range from 1-1/2" to 1-3/4". They are approximately 3/4" to 1" thick. This is not set in stone, as again we are using those precious little cut-offs and scraps and will adjust our shape and sizes according to the material used.

The rare-earth magnets I'm using are 1/2" diameter by 1/8" thick. I have drilled a hole with a 1/2" Fostner bit, as this creates a flat bottom hole. One of the easy ways of handling these magnets is on a scale or ruler, as shown here.

With the magnet mounted on the scale it is very easy to place it in the hole and slide the scale away. If you put the scale back again, the magnet will immediately jump to it and can be easily removed from the hole. While the magnet is attached to your scale it will also stick to the lathe, so you can attach both to the lathe, keeping them handy.

Remove the blank and put in a scrap block. I am starting to true up the scrap block and make a tenon to fit into the magnet's hole. This is going to end up being a jam chuck to support and drive our work piece, which will hold the magnet body concentric to the drilled hole.

Make sure the face is flat and, as a precaution, that the magnet is recessed slightly below it. This will ensure that after being glued in it does not scratch anything it may come into contact with. When this is accomplished, sand the face and apply the finish of your choice. I will be using Deft™ satin finish again.

An easy way to size the tenon is to put a small angle on the very end and, with the lathe running, lightly hold the work piece to the tenon.

This will cause a friction burn at the end, showing you the diameter you have to cut the tenon to. Work slowly, you want to have a tight fit.

Be sure that the length of the tenon does not bottom out in the hole as we want the face to be in contact with the larger diameter of the scrap block.

The tenon completed.

The face of the scrap block should be flat, as this will help to keep the work piece from rocking, which will, in turn, help to make a secure hold. If your fit is not tight enough, you can put double-face tape between the flat surfaces to help hold the work piece.

Bring up the tailstock with a live center. If you do not have a blunt or flat tip for your center, put a piece of scrap between the work piece and the tip. This will protect the wood. If your work piece is thicker than necessary, this step may not be needed as you may be cutting away the part that would be damaged by the live center point.

Progress.

Starting to shape our magnet body.

Adding embellishment to the magnet body. Keep in mind that you do have a hole in the middle. If you go too deep, you will find that out the hard way. Remember, I warned you!

Continuing to shape, refining the form.

Pull back the tailstock and lightly work the top.

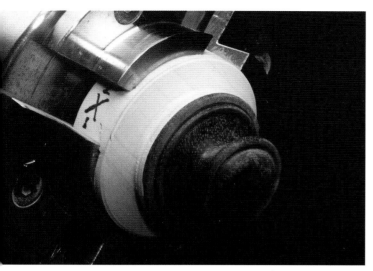

The magnet body is turned and ready for sanding.

Again I have drilled a 5/8" hole with a Fostner bit and made a new jam chuck to match. Before removing from the chuck, sand and finish the bottom.

Our completed piece, sanded and finished. All that's left to do is glue in the magnet using either epoxy, silicone adhesive, or flexible cyanoacrylate.

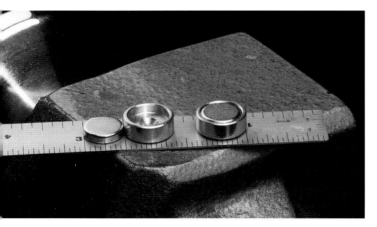

Starting to shape the magnet body to acquire our form.

For our next magnet, the wood will be bocote and we are going to use a steel cup in conjunction with the magnet—this increases its power directionally. It also means we will have to drill a larger hole due to the steel cup. The magnet goes inside the steel cup and is held there by its magnetic attraction. This magnet will also have a new design element—a captive ring. A captive ring is a ring formed and cut free between two larger diameters, which totally traps it. This always gets a "how did you do that?"

Forming the bead for the captive ring.

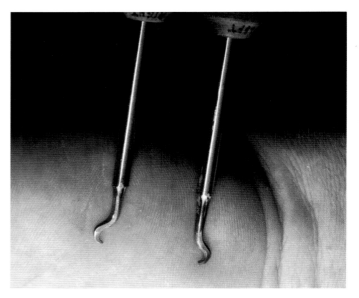

Commercial ring tools are available, but I chose to make mine because they do what I desire them to. Being smaller in stature, they will go into places the commercial ones will not. I made these from dental picks attained at a flea market. I put a metal rod the diameter that I wanted into a vise, then heated the dental pick and, with a pair of pliers, wrapped it around the rod. This established the radius. I designed mine where I needed a left and a right. The two tools have to be made as a pair, as the right one will go from the right hand side half way around the ring and the left will do the same on the left hand side. The care used when making these dictates how good the captive ring is that they will produce. I did not reharden the dental picks as I would rather have them bend than shatter if a mistake is made.

Using a parting tool, go down along each side in order to establish the width and provide tool clearance for your captive ring. Remember, we have drilled a larger hole in this one so we have even less stock to work with.

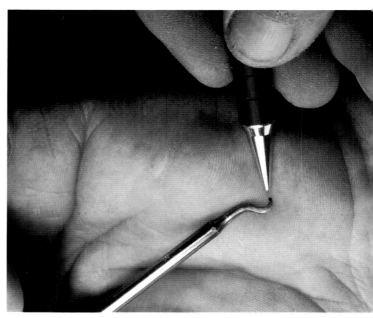

When making the tools, the only area that cuts is the leading edge where my pencil is pointing. It is sharpened in a scraper manner. This is the reason there is a left and right. All the rest of the surfaces have had the edges broken to make sure they do not cut, as their purpose is follow around the ring and we do not want them to cut.

We have cleaned up the ring and are ready to sand it, prior to cutting it free. If you make the mistake of cutting the ring free before sanding, it will become a very tedious job. One time will teach you.

Following around the bead and starting to undercut it.

When making captive rings, especially in this position, the end grain can have cracks (or pores that act as cracks), which would allow the ring to break. A simple precaution is to flood the ring with the thin cyanoacrylate to eliminate the possibility. This will also help to strengthen the ring.

Work both sides back and forth towards the center of the ring until it is cut free.

Pull back the tailstock and shape the top.

We now have to hold the ring aside and work out the surface below it to a pleasing contour.

Hold the ring aside and sand the area underneath it. Finish sanding the rest of the piece

I am decorating slightly with beads, trying not to be overpowering.

When your sanding is complete, apply finish, remove from the lathe, put the magnet in the cup, and glue it into your piece.

Switch Knobs

This project came out of necessity. The knob pictured here was given to me by my father. Being elderly and having arthritis, both of my parents were having trouble turning a lamp on and off because of the small diameter of the knob. Dad had made this one up, used it, found that it worked, and asked me to make more for the rest of their lamps. Since I am always reminded that he taught me everything I know, he turned the project over to me. Yes, I could have replaced the rotating sockets with push sockets, but there are also three way switches and old lamps that, while they have no monetary value, are valued as keepsakes.

Don't sell these knobs short. After making them up and showing them to friends, I nearly depleted the stock I had ready for this book. Which, of course, meant more work for me. But replacing them let me use my imagination and helped me to fine tune the knobs. I was then challenged to do different things with them. I started to combine different materials and make mini works of art instead of just plain knobs. In other words, I was having fun with it. As with any project, you are limited only by your own imagination. Let it flow. Now it's time to "turn and rotate" an oversized therapeutic switch knob.

For this project we are going to be using a drill chuck in the headstock. The main downfall of a Morse taper is vibration. Vibration will knock anything loose, including a Morse taper. Any time we do this, it is best to have a draw bolt. The draw bolt goes through the spindle and screws into the end of the chuck's Morse taper. By using the draw bolt, it is impossible for the chuck to come loose. This is a safety precaution. If your chuck does not have a tapped hole in the end of the Morse taper, a competent machine shop can do this for you. Any time you are using a drill chuck in the headstock, no matter what the project, having the machining done is far cheaper than going to your dentist and having bridgework made.

I normally use a small gouge to cut the plastic knob in preparation for gluing it in. A straight 3/8" plug cutter would do the same thing if you were making multiple knobs.

Put the plastic knob into the chuck and hand tighten. The end that is going to be glued into the wood is tapered. This probably would have no effect on the gluing, but being me I prefer to have it parallel.

Turning the tapered end to a parallel diameter.

I'm making mine 3/8" diameter. Again, this is not etched in stone—you can do whatever suits you. If you do not want to take the time to turn it down or deem it unnecessary, drill a hole large enough to accommodate the end of the plastic knob and fill with epoxy or a glue of your choice.

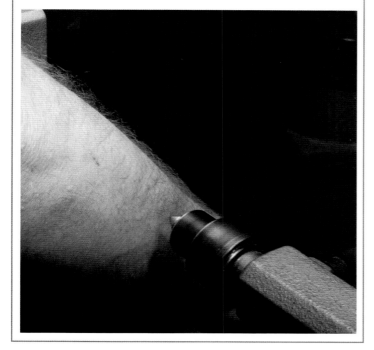

Since my plastic knob was turned to 3/8" diameter, I am using a 3/8" Fostner bit, as it will create a flat bottom hole. Drill deep enough to be able to seat the knob just below the surface of the wood, to allow for clean up.

Put some medium density cyanoacrylate into the hole and seat the plastic knob inside. Using the center point on your live center in the tailstock, bring it forward into the threaded hole of the knob. This will help keep it aligned to the work piece. Hit with accelerator.

Put a piece of wood of your choice into a four jaw chuck, or whatever means you prefer to hold it by, and clean up the surface. The piece I am using happens to be a scrap of cherry burl.

Clean up the back side and sand.

Remove your piece from the four jaw chuck and put the drill chuck back into the headstock with the draw bolt attached. Put the knob end into the drill chuck and hand tighten. Make sure that the cleaned up surface is tight against the face of the jaws, as this will help support the piece while turning. You can put the live center up against it for support. This will give you a little extra support but don't penetrate below your finished surface. Start to clean up and shape your knob.

Since there is not much supporting the work, vibration is a problem. Here I am using my fingers to back up my cut and dampen vibration. A light touch is mandatory.

Remove the tailstock and finish the face of your knob. Remember the purpose of this knob and don't make it too small, as arthritic fingers have a hard time grabbing small objects.

Finish your decoration of the knob. Work carefully. We don't want our wooden portion to look like it was hewn with an axe, as given that no one has seen it before it's going to come under close scrutiny. Finish accordingly.

Sanding the knob.

Slightly loosen the chuck and pull the knob out a short distance, then retighten by hand. This is done to allow us to get finish on the back side of the knob.

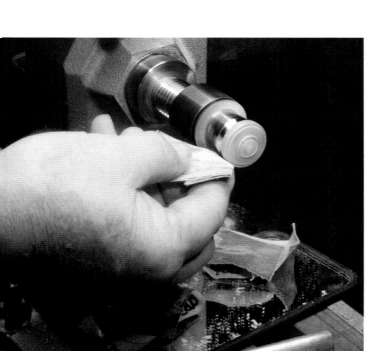

Don't forget, this is a great spot to use that mirror.

Hey Dad — your project is complete. Thanks for the neat idea.

Brushes

All of our projects so far have basically been faceplate oriented. We should make a clean sweep and throw in a spindle project—you should be familiar with this after having turned pens. The basic difference will be adding contours and beads to put together an eye pleasing form designed to hold a bunch of hog bristles. This little brush can be used for a multitude of purposes. It can be used to keep surfaces such as computer keyboards, plants, or carvings clean of dust and debris, or for whatever purpose you need it. You can once again use those odd bits of wood for a lasting gift that won't be brushed aside.

One of the things that I do is use a cone dead center in the headstock to drive the work piece. Before live centers, a cone dead center was the method used to support the work piece in the tailstock. They had to be waxed to provide lubrication so the wood would not burn, etc. Live centers have replaced this method. To use the dead center in the headstock, you also need a live center, preferably with a cone tip, in the tailstock. If you use a sharp pointed tip instead of the cone, you will have a tendency to split the blank as you apply pressure necessary to drive the work. The beauty of this setup is that it is driven strictly by friction. If you do have a catch or even something worse, the work piece will stop for lack of driving power, rather than possibly splitting, which would be normal with a four-pronged positive drive.

First select your blank. This one happens to be cocobolo. Make sure you have sufficient stock to be able to drill the proper diameter hole for the bristles. Mine is 1" square and I will be drilling a 5/8" hole in the end of the blank to accommodate the bristle tufts. Mark off the center of the blank at the tailstock end and bring up the tailstock to help align the blank while tightening the chuck. This should keep it in alignment as best as possible when drilling. Now using a 5/8" Fostner drill bit, bore a hole in the end of the blank, approximately 3/4" deep. All we need the hole depth for is to cover the ends of the bristle where they are glued together. Any other variation would be a design choice.

Now that we have bored a hole in the end of our brush blank, we need a means of supporting it. I have set up a piece of hardwood between centers. I am going to turn a 5/8" diameter plug, which will go into the hole that we drilled in the end of the blank. Not only will this support the end, it will also allow us to make a thinner wall in the brush area, allowing better design options.

Turn the lathe on and advance the tailstock. Hold the live center from turning while the lathe is running. Make sure the work piece is rotating. Slowly advance the tailstock and burn in a good depression with the tip.

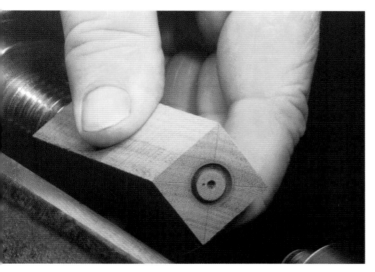

This depression, being cut into the wood, will make a more positive location on the live center and help maintain concentricity.

With a roughing gouge, or whatever gouge you have, reduce to a cylinder.

With a skew, reduce the cylinder down to 5/8". The better the fit, the less play and chance of vibration during turning.

Our cylinder has been reduced to its proper diameter and we are going to cut it off, creating a plug to go inside the drilled hole on the blank.

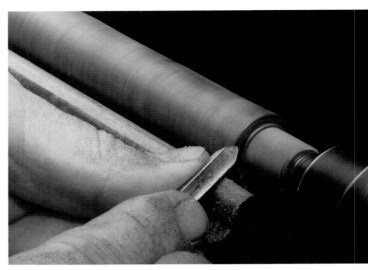

Face off the end so you have a clean surface on the brush end.

Take the dead center out of the headstock and replace it with the four jaw chuck and drilled blank. Insert the plug and bring up your tailstock. This method – the blank being held in a chuck—will be make it easier to turn small diameters as we do not need the tailstock to provide pressure to drive it. Normally, by applying pressure it is easy to set up a vibration. If you don't have a four jaw chuck, you could drive it normally between centers with the plug positioned in the hole in the blank.

Starting at the tailstock end, begin to shape the handle. Always start at the farthest position from your driving force, which is the headstock.

Reduce the blank to a cylinder.

Progress on the handle.

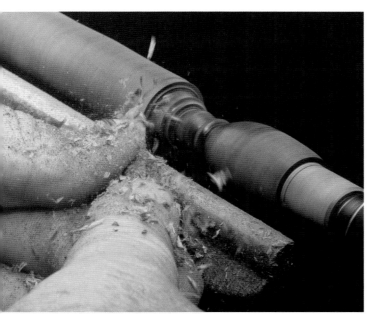

Continued shaping.

Now that our detailing is completed, we will start moving towards the headstock, making the rest of the handle. I'm using a roughing gouge.

Here I'm rolling a bead with the spindle gouge to continue the design. Since we want the brush to have a delicate look to it rather than look like something that would sweep cement, spend a little time and make some beads or other designs of your choice. Since this area is reduced in diameter, we want to finish up before moving towards the headstock, as vibration could become a factor. As you shape the part that holds the brush, remember you have a hole in it. Strive to make good clean cuts—unless sanding is one of your favorite pastimes.

As I work the diameter of our handle down, I am supporting the work piece with my fingers. I'm applying the same pressure with my supporting hand as I am with the tool. If I were pressing too hard with the tool, you would see a wisp of smoke curl off my fingers and they would be medium well done in no time, so this is a light control situation.

Progress on the lower portion of the handle.

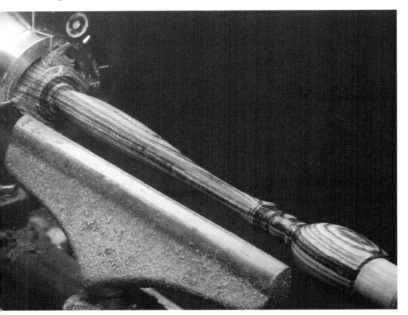

Now that we have all the detail cut, it's time to sand.

Sanding the brush.

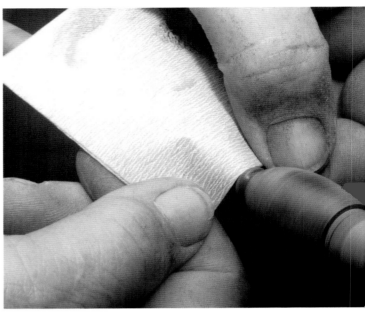

If you've taken the time to put in clean, crisp detail, take the time to sand properly. Sand up to the beads with the edge of the sandpaper, don't just roll over them. We want to keep our crispness in the detail.

When you have finished sanding, shut the lathe off and sand in the direction of the grain. This will eliminate concentric sanding marks. Finish with Deft™ or the finish of your choice.

Shape the end of the handle close to the desired shape.

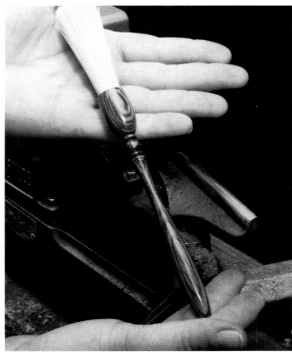

Remove the plug from the end. After the brush is well dried, buff with a little wax and glue the bristle tufts in with epoxy. The tufts can be purchased from woodworking suppliers or craft stores.

Supporting the handle so it does not get away, take a skew and cut through the remaining nubbin. If needed, trim off the very end by hand with a knife, then sand and apply a little finish.

The Gallery

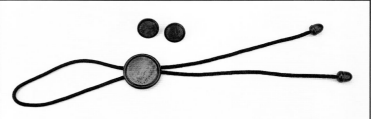

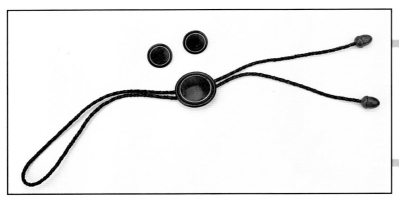

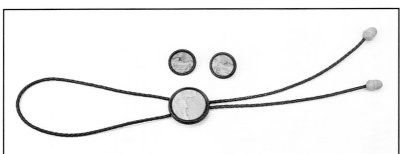

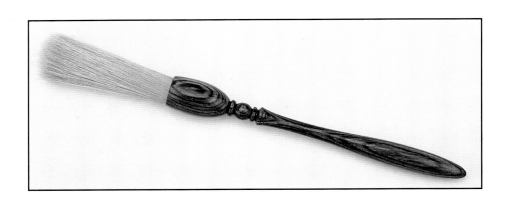